IMAGES
of America

BOONESBOROUGH

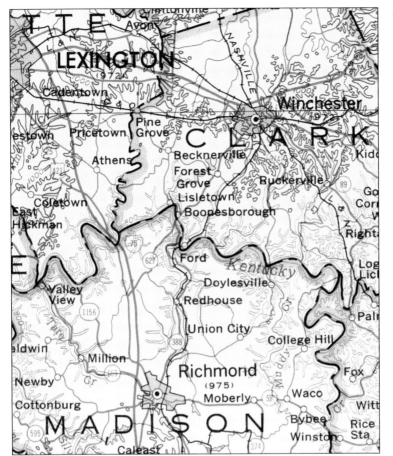

This section of a 1973 topographic map of Kentucky shows Boonesborough on the Kentucky River situated on the road from Winchester in Clark County to Richmond in Madison County. Daniel Boone piloted a group of settlers here in 1775, and the Transylvania Company erected Fort Boonesborough. (Author's collection.)

IMAGES
of America

BOONESBOROUGH

Harry G. Enoch

ARCADIA
PUBLISHING

Published by Arcadia Publishing
Charleston, South Carolina

Printed in the United States of America

Library of Congress Control Number: 2023938093

For all general information, please contact Arcadia Publishing:
Telephone 843-853-2070
Fax 843-853-0044
E-mail sales@arcadiapublishing.com

Visit us on the Internet at www.arcadiapublishing.com

*To the employees and volunteers at Fort Boonesborough State Park
whose efforts make the history of Boonesborough come alive.*

CONTENTS

ACKNOWLEDGMENTS

I am deeply indebted to a number of individuals without whose help this work would not have been possible. A special thanks are due to Dean Whitaker, president of the Society of Boonesborough; Jack Winburn, manager of Fort Boonesborough State Park; Jackie Couture, head of Special Collections and Archives at Eastern Kentucky University; and Rick Allen, Walters family historian. I am also extremely grateful for the assistance of Robert A. Powell, Sandy Stults, Julie Morgan, Vicki Whitaker, George and Elizabeth Chalfant, Jenimarie Sowers, Diana Neely, Susie Rickert, Randell Jones, John Fox, Kathy Cummings, Ken Kamper, Bill Berryman, Kristen Good, Sarah Coblentz, Will Hodgkin, Jeff Cress, Nona Cress, Mike Flynn, Mary Beth Hendricks, Bob Tabor, Deborah Garrison, Anne Crabb, and my wife, Clare Sipple.

The following abbreviations are used to acknowledge the sources of photographs in this work.

AC	Author's collection
BT	Bob Tabor, Winchester
CMHA	Carol M. Highsmith Archive, Library of Congress, Prints and Photographs Division
CNCT	Carlisle-Nicholas Co. Tourism
COE	US Army Corps of Engineers, Louisville District
DWC	Dean Whitaker Collection of Daniel Boone–related photographs and memorabilia
ECP	Estill Curtis Pennington, Paris
EKU	Special Collections and Archives, Eastern Kentucky University, Richmond
HABS	Historic American Building Survey, Stanley P. Mixon, photographer, Library of Congress, Prints and Photographs Division
JF	Dr. John Fox, president, Friends of Boone Trace
KK	Ken Kamper, Daniel Boone historian
KLO	Kentucky Land Office, Kentucky Secretary of State, Frankfort
KRWW	Kentucky River Watershed Watch, Frankfort
LOC	Library of Congress, Prints and Photographs Division
MCOB	Madison County Order Books, Madison County Courthouse, Richmond
MF	Maurice Flynn, Clark County
MLKAM	Mildred Lane Kemper Art Museum, Washington University, St. Louis, Missouri
NC	Nona Cress, Morrow, Ohio
NOH	Neal O. Hammon, Shelby County
NPG	National Portrait Gallery, Smithsonian Institution
RAP	Robert A. Powell, Kentucky artist
RJ	Randell Jones, DanielBooneFootsteps.com
VW	Vicki Whitaker, Richmond
WFC	Dr. David J. Williams family collection of photographs and memorabilia
WFP	Walters family photographs
WH	Will Hodgkin, Winchester
WSPC	Winchester Sun Photograph Collection, Bluegrass Heritage Museum

INTRODUCTION

Boonesborough holds a storied place in America's history. Kentucky is often referred to as the place where the Western Movement began. In 1775, Col. Richard Henderson's Transylvania Company purchased a large tract of land from the Cherokee Indians that included much of present-day Kentucky. Boonesborough became the headquarters for the land company and, at that time, was the center of western migration from the 13 original colonies.

The company hired Daniel Boone to blaze a route from Sycamore Shoals in Tennessee to the Kentucky River, where Fort Boonesborough was erected. A noted hunter and frontiersman in his day, Daniel Boone has since become an American icon. After John Filson published his "Adventures of Col. Daniel Boon" in 1784, Boone became an international sensation. Repeating the myth that Boone removed to Missouri after losing all of his Kentucky lands ("unable to call a single acre his own"), contemporary biographers often paint him as an uneducated rube done in by crafty lawyers and his own failure to understand complex land laws. Research by the late Neal Hammon proves differently. Boone was well-versed in the land acquisition process and made a good living as a surveyor. He also profited handsomely from the sale of lands he owned. In addition to being a successful businessman, Boone rose to the rank of colonel in the militia and served several terms in the Virginia Assembly. As Hammon concluded, "After 1780 he was generally wealthy by pioneer standards and a well-known and respected leader in the communities where he lived."

In 1775, land-hungry easterners began flocking to Kentucky by way of Cumberland Gap and found refuge at Fort Boonesborough, while they explored the country. Boonesborough is often remembered as the site of two iconic events—the capture and rescue of the Boone and Callaway girls in 1776 and a siege by Chief Blackfish and his 400 Shawnee warriors successfully repelled in 1778. In recognition of the latter, the National Park Service designated Fort Boonesborough a Revolutionary War Battlefield.

By 1784, the Indian threat had diminished, and the fort was dismantled. The Virginia Legislature issued a charter to the town of Boonesborough in 1779. Although the community eventually faded away, the location would later become a tourist destination.

Boonesborough is recognized as the site of the first legislative session and the first religious service held in Kentucky. In 1840, the first Boonesborough celebration was organized to honor the establishment of Kentucky's first settlement. (Later, it was proven that Harrodsburg was actually Kentucky's first settlement.) Among those honored were Keziah Callaway French and her enslaved servant Dolly, who had resided at the old fort. In 1907, the Boonesborough Chapter of the Daughters of the American Revolution placed a Pioneer Monument at the site of the original fort. The National Park Service designated Fort Boonesborough a National Historic Landmark in 1996.

Boonesborough was the site of Kentucky's first ferry. The Virginia Assembly awarded a charter to Richard Callaway in 1779. Callaway and several others were killed by Indians while building a ferry boat. The first boat, called a "cable ferry," was pulled across the river by a cable attached to each bank. In the 20th century, ferries were towed across the river by sternwheel tugboats. The ferry, which provided a critical link on the road between Winchester and Richmond, operated under a series of owners until a bridge was erected across the Kentucky River in 1931. The original bridge was replaced with a modern span in 1994.

In 1917, after years of unsuccessful starts, the US Army Corps of Engineers completed a series of 14 locks and dams along 255 miles of the Kentucky River. Lock and Dam 10 at Boonesborough were completed in 1905. The Walters family, John and John Jr., served as lockmasters from 1906 until 1975. Although the envisioned growth of commercial traffic on the Kentucky River failed to materialize, the locks and dams served two important and unexpected purposes. The locks saw considerable traffic from recreational users and helped establish Boonesborough as a tourist destination before they closed in 1994. More importantly, the dams impounded bodies of water that were tapped for municipal water supplies. The pool behind dam 10 serves as the principal water source for the city of Winchester. The Corps of Engineers deeded Lock and Dam 10 to the state of Kentucky in 1996.

The year lock and dam 10 were completed a wave of ice and saw logs crashed into the dam and gouged a new path around it requiring expensive repairs. However, the breach uncovered a fine sand beach just below the dam that became a magnet for locals and tourists. In 1909, Dr. David J. Williams purchased the tract of land that included the beach and original fort site. Here, he opened the Boonesboro Beach Resort that eventually included a hotel, tourist cottages, a restaurant, a dance hall, and bathhouses.

Leaders in Clark and Madison Counties lobbied the state of Kentucky for decades to take over the resort. The state finally acquired this property and 1965 saw the dedication of Fort Boonesborough State Park. In 1976, the park was expanded with the construction of a replica fort, an expanded area for RV and tent campers, and a boat dock. The completed fort featured cabins, blockhouses, furnishings, and pioneer craftspersons in period costumes. The state also built a new highway (KY 627) that provided convenient access to the park from Interstates 64 and 75. For many years, Fort Boonesborough stood out as the most popular attraction in Kentucky's state park system. A swimming pool was added in 1993, and the Kentucky River Museum opened in 2002.

The Boonesborough area counts numerous other historic places along the Kentucky River. Another fortress, Fort Boonesboro, was erected by the Union army on the Clark County side during the Civil War to protect the important river crossing. The nearby town of Ford began with the booming lumber industry, but after the mills closed, the town reverted to a sleepy village. The area also features Lower Howard's Creek Nature & Heritage Preserve. The creek valley, which had been one of Kentucky's earliest industrial areas, today serves as a habitat for threatened plant and animal species. A new Kentucky Scenic Byway opened in 2020 on Athens-Boonesboro Road. The route begins across the river from Fort Boonesborough and continues seven miles to Athens, where Daniel Boone established Boone Station in 1779. Over the years, floods created havoc up and down the river. Recreational boating has been decimated, as many of the old boat docks washed away. In spite of nature's forces, two boat docks survive today along with several popular restaurants and, of course, Fort Boonesborough State Park.

A note on the spelling of Boonesborough may be helpful. The postal service was responsible for modernizing many place names in the 1800s, including "Boonesboro." That led to some places adopting the new spelling (such as Boonesboro Beach Resort) while some retained the old (Fort Boonesborough State Park).

One

DANIEL BOONE

In the summer of 1820, Chester Harding set out to visit the famous pioneer in Missouri. Although initially reluctant to pose for a painting, after his daughter Jemima's prodding, the modest Boone agreed. Harding then completed the only life portrait ever made of Col. Daniel Boone just a few weeks before the legendary frontiersman's death. Harding produced a number of copies of his painting, including this version at the National Portrait Gallery. (NPG.)

Daniel's father, Squire Boone, immigrated to Pennsylvania from the small town of Bradninch, England. In 1731, he built a one-and-a-half-story log house in the Oley Valley near present-day Reading in Berks County where Daniel was born, the sixth of eleven children. The home was later expanded to a two-story house, now owned by the Pennsylvania Historical and Museum Commission. (HABS.)

Boone's first entrance into Kentucky was through Cumberland Gap, an easily accessible opening in the Cumberland Mountain massif. This Civil War view from the south side of the gap shows the withdrawal of the Confederate army in 1863. The gap is located near the Kentucky, Virginia, and Tennessee borders. (LOC.)

The large oil painting entitled *Daniel Boone's Arrival in Kentucky* was created by Works Progress Administration (WPA) artist Ward Lockwood during Roosevelt's New Deal in 1938. The painting portrays Boone and five companions dressed in buckskin and carrying long rifles emerging from a dense woodland. Boone's coonskin cap is uncharacteristic, as he preferred a traditional beaver hat. The mural can be viewed in the main courtroom on the second floor of the US post office and US courthouse at the corner of Limestone and Barr Streets in Lexington. Lockwood's mural hangs on the wall opposite the judicial bench. Photographer Carol M. Highsmith included this mural in her work documenting significant Boone locations throughout the United States. (CMHA.)

William Tylee Ranney's painting commemorates Boone's first visit to Kentucky in 1769. According to John Filson's *Adventures of Col. Daniel Boon*, "On the seventh day of June from the top of an eminence, we saw with pleasure the beautiful level of Kentucke." The scene depicts Boone (arm extended) on Pilot Knob in Powell County with his companions John Finley, John Stewart, Joseph Holden, James Monay, and William Cool. (ECP.)

On his first visit to Kentucky, Boone found himself surrounded by Indians and leaped off a cliff to escape. There are many versions of this story, but none are reliable. This old postcard depicts one of the supposed locations, a palisade on the Kentucky River less than a mile downstream from Boonesborough. (DWC.)

In the popular imagination, Daniel Boone was a rugged frontiersman who conquered the wilderness with his superior woodcraft and hunting skills. In reality, Boone was a more rounded individual. He served as a militia commander and civil officer in Fayette County, Virginia, and was elected to several terms in the Virginia Legislature. Boone prospered financially in Kentucky by virtue of the income he derived from land surveying. (AC.)

William Bush became friends with Boone back in Virginia and came to Kentucky with Boone in 1775. Bush resided at Boonesborough until 1784 and spent much time marking land claims in present-day Clark County. Boone surveyed 11 tracts of land for Bush that came to be known as the Bush Settlement. (AC.)

Survey for Andrew Tribble, 500 Acres of Land by Virtue of Treasury Warrant duly Entred N.º 4028 Situate Lying & being in the County of Fayette upon the Waters of Howards Lower Creek beginning at (A) a White Oak Sugar tree & Elm In Robert McMullions line thence S.66 W. 117 poles to (B) one Sugar thence S.55 W. 50 poles to (C) Black Walnut & Sugar tree thence S.46 E. 520 to (D) Black Walnut & Sugar tree thence N.44 E. 164 poles to two Sugar tree in Thomas Browns Line to (E) thence N.46 W. 460 poles passing S.d McMullions Corner to the begining at (A)

James Stevins }
Phillip Bush } Chain men

Daniel Boone D.S.F.C.

William Bush Landmarker & pilot

Jany 1.st 1783

Be.g Cont.g 500 Acres

Platted from a Scale of 200 p.s to 1 inch

Virginia had a three-step process for obtaining a fee-simple title to land in Kentucky. One first had to acquire a "warrant" or entitlement to the land. Second, a survey plat had to be made by an official surveyor. Finally, after the warrant and survey were returned to Virginia, the governor issued a patent. This plat is for a 1783 survey of 500 acres on Lower Howard's Creek that Boone ran for Rev. Andrew Tribble in the Bush Settlement. The chain carriers were James Stevens and Phillip Bush; William Bush served as pilot and marker. Surveys were made by the "metes and bounds" method—corners were marked on trees and courses were described by compass direction and distance (south 55 degrees west, 50 poles). This land was then in Fayette County, now Clark County. The author resides on part of the tract. (KLO.)

Boone was a large landholder in Kentucky. The first step in acquiring land was obtaining a land warrant issued by the state of Virginia. In this example, Boone paid 800 pounds for a treasury warrant in 1781 for the right to patent 500 acres of land. He sold the warrant to his son-in-law William Hays. (KLO.)

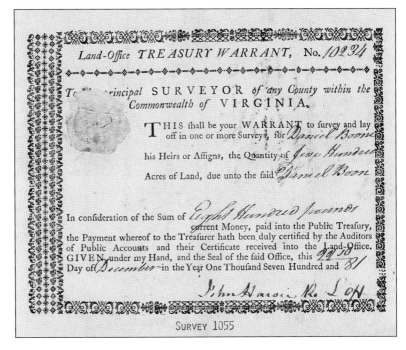

Always the wanderer, Boone settled his family in several different Kentucky locations. From Boonesborough they moved to Boone's Station near Athens (1779). In 1783, they relocated to Limestone (now Maysville) where Boone kept a trading post. Their last home in Kentucky was this cabin on Brushy Fork in Nicholas County (1795). In 1799, Boone moved to Missouri with his extended family. (CNCT.)

Daniel spent his last years living with his youngest son, Nathan. In the summer of 1800, Nathan built a log house and, several years later, replaced it with a stone building. Daniel died here surrounded by family on September 26, 1820. Located in St. Charles County, Missouri, the "Historic Daniel Boone Home at Lindenwood Park" is operated by the county's parks and recreation department. (KK.)

Daniel Boone was buried beside Rebecca near Marthasville, Missouri. In 1845, a delegation from Kentucky secured permission to disinter Daniel and his wife and move their remains to the Frankfort Cemetery. The monument was completed in 1860 and restored in 1910. The site has a commanding view of the Kentucky River valley. Some evidence suggests that the Kentuckians moved the wrong bodies. (CMHA.)

On June 2, 1910, Kentucky's new capitol was dedicated. The capitol exterior is faced in Indiana limestone and Vermont granite, while the interior features generous use of white Georgia marble, gray Tennessee marble, and dark green Italian marble. Decorative lunettes above each staircase highlight the entrances to the House and Senate chambers. Painted in oils by T. Gilbert White, both depict frontier scenes with Daniel Boone. The east mural (above) portrays Boone and his party catching their first glimpse of the Bluegrass region atop Pilot Knob in 1769. The west mural depicts negotiations at the Treaty of Sycamore Shoals, which led to the purchase of Cherokee land that would eventually become Kentucky. (Both, EKU.)

BICENTENNIAL
CELEBRATION

OF

DANIEL BOONE (1734-1934)

BY

The Commonwealth of Kentucky
At the Site of Fort Boonesborough

Monday, September 3, 1934
Daniel Boone The Prince of Pioneers

Fort Boonesborough
Erected by the Transylvania Company

Col. Nathaniel Hart, Col. Richard Henderson
Founders

First Fortified Station West of the Alleghenies. The first legislative body assembled here west of the Alleghenies. Withstood three sieges, Daniel Boone in Command. First religious service held here west of Alleghenies by the Rev. Mr. Lythe. The largest and best built stockade and stood for the defense of all smaller forts. A National Monument in 1934.

Compliments of

The Boonesborough Chapter D. A. R.

Mrs. Christopher D. Chenault, Founder, 1896
Mrs. Charles A. Keith, Regent
Miss Florence Burnam, Secretary
Mrs. James W. Caperton, Chairman
Boonesborough Monument Committee

This broadside was prepared for the 1934 bicentennial celebration of Daniel Boone's birth. While events occurred throughout the year, the principal festivities were held at Boonesborough on Labor Day, September 3. More than 6,000 persons were in attendance. Judge Samuel Wilson of Lexington, chairman of the Daniel Boone Bicentennial Commission, presided over the assembly. Speakers included a number of Kentucky officials, including Gov. Ruby Laffoon, US senator Alben W. Barkley, and Congressman Virgil Chapman. A number of lineal descendants of Daniel Boone were introduced, as were representatives of the American Order of Pioneers and the Boone Family Association. Members of the Bicentennial Commission held a luncheon for dignitaries at the Boonesboro Beach Resort. A picnic lunch was served in Sycamore Hollow, and the Madison County Historical Society conducted hourly tours of historic spots. (DWC.)

The Daniel Boone Commemorative Coin was authorized by the US Congress in honor of Boone's 200th birthday. Sculptor Henry Augustus Lukeman designed the coin, and the Philadelphia Mint produced the silver half dollars in 1934. These 50¢ pieces have become valuable collectors' items with the uncirculated 1934 version selling for thousands of dollars today. (DWC.)

The US Postal Service honored Daniel Boone with a 6¢ commemorative stamp as part of their American Folklore Series. It was issued on September 26, 1968, at Frankfort where Boone is buried. The stamp pictures a rifle, powder horn, and knife on a wooden board. The pipe tomahawk is a reminder of Boone's adoption by Chief Blackfish into the Shawnee Indian tribe. (DWC.)

The nine-foot-tall Daniel Boone statue was originally sculpted in plaster by Enid Yandell for exhibit by The Filson Club of Louisville in the Kentucky Building at the 1893 World's Fair in Chicago. In 1906, a bronze cast of the statue was installed in Cherokee Park, Louisville. Eastern Kentucky University president Robert R. Martin received permission from Louisville officials to send the statue to the Modern Art Foundry in Long Island, New York, for a replica to be made. This second bronze cast made in 1967 was installed on the EKU campus in Richmond. The statue, located in front of the Keen Johnson Building, weighs about 3,500 pounds and is now green with age. It has long been a campus tradition among faculty, students, and alumni to rub Boone's foot for luck, leaving the toe of his left shoe a bright bronze gold. (EKU.)

This larger-than-life portrait of Daniel Boone was commissioned for the Fort Boonesborough dedication in 1974. The artist, Jack Hodgkin, painted Boone in buckskin with his long rifle and powder horn. His model was Johnny B. Allman, son of the legendary Johnny Allman who built Allman's Restaurant on the Kentucky River. The portrait hangs in the fort museum today. (WSPC.)

Scott New was the first to portray Daniel Boone for the Kentucky Humanities Council's Chautauqua program. His first-person interpretation of the pioneer was wildly successful with schoolchildren and adult audiences. Scott, formerly an interpreter and historian at Fort Boonesborough State Park, also played Boone in several film productions and posed as Boone in artist David Wright's painting *Cumberland Gap*, on display at the Cumberland Gap National Historic Park. (RJ.)

Fess Parker starred in the hugely popular TV series *Daniel Boone* that aired 165 episodes on NBC from 1964 to 1970. In 1968, Parker gave the commencement address at Eastern Kentucky University (EKU) and was awarded an honorary doctorate degree. EKU president Robert Martin took Parker to visit the "real Boonesborough," shown here at the Pioneer Monument at Fort Boonesborough State Park. (EKU.)

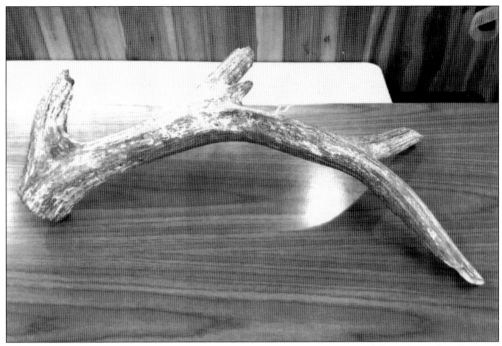

This elk antler bears the carving "D. Boon 1778," and possibly a faint "e" at the end of "Boon." Donated to the Fort Boonesborough Foundation in 2017, the antler was carbon-dated to the late 18th century. Since his death in 1820, dozens of Boone signatures have surfaced on rifles, powder horns, and other items, as well as rocks and trees. Very few have been authenticated. (DWC.)

The fascination in Kentucky with everything Daniel Boone lives on. Countless monuments, paintings, statues, and other works of art are still being turned out. This 10-inch square bust of Daniel Boone carved by Berea College professor Bert Mullins, a noted artist, muralist, and woodcarver, is on display at the Eastern Kentucky University Archives in Richmond. (VW.)

In 2017, Fort Boonesborough State Park held an exhibit of Daniel Boone memorabilia that represented a lifetime of collecting by Ray Buckberry of Bowling Green. When the collection grew too large for Buckberry's home, he donated it to the state park. Items, which can be viewed by park visitors, include coloring books, and lunch boxes from the Fess Parker TV series, prints, posters, puzzles, children's toys, coffee mugs, and more. (DWC.)

The statue of Daniel Boone, dedicated in 1933, stood at the entrance to the Boonesborough Bridge for many years. Created by A D. Fisher, it depicted Boone as a short stocky figure that many found implausible. The statue was moved a short distance when Ford Road was rebuilt in the 1960s. Construction of the new bridge in 1994 forced another move, this time to College Park in Winchester. (WSPC.)

Two

FORT BOONESBOROUGH

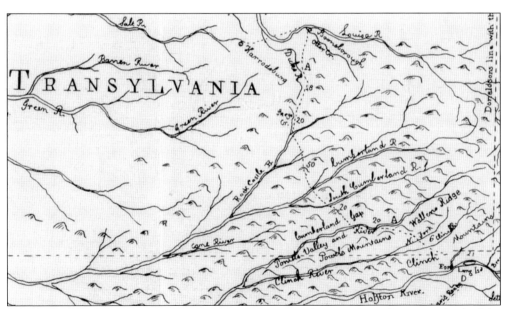

In March 1775, Daniel Boone led a party of about 30 road cutters from the Long Island of the Holston (now Kingsport, Tennessee) to establish a settlement on the Kentucky River. On this detail of a rare map ("New Settlement Called Transilvania," 1776), the dashed line marks the route of Boone Trace ending at Boonesborough. Harrodsburg, the only other settlement in Kentucky at that time, is also shown. (AC.)

Colonel Richard Henderson
1735 - 1785
" The Political Father of Kentucky "

Col. Richard Henderson of North Carolina formed the Transylvania Company with a group of investors. They signed a treaty with the Cherokees at Sycamore Shoals (present-day Elizabethton, Tennessee) acquiring some 20 million acres of land in Kentucky and Tennessee for 10,000 pounds sterling in trade goods. Henderson and two of the proprietors, Nathaniel Hart and John Luttrell, followed Boone's party to Kentucky. (DWC.)

Henderson's party stopped at Martin's Station, the last outpost of civilization in 1775, and stored their wagons before continuing on to Boonesborough. The reconstructed station shown here is an outdoor living history museum at Wilderness Road State Park in Lee County, Virginia. The original station was near Rose Hill, a few miles east. (RJ.)

On March 25, 1775, Daniel Boone's advance party was surprised by the Indians who killed Capt. William Twitty and his slave Sam, and badly wounded Felix Walker. Although only about 15 miles from their final destination on the Kentucky River, the company had to put up a small fortification, called "Fort Twetty" on the marker, where they could tend to Walker until he recovered enough to travel. (VW.)

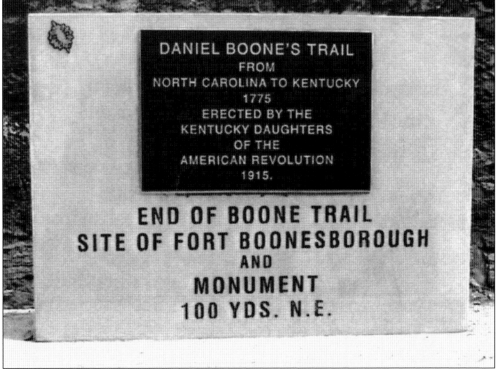

In 1915, the Boonesborough Chapter of the Daughters of the American Revolution (DAR) erected a monument marking the end of Boone Trace at Fort Boonesborough. The marker was originally placed at the edge of the old Richmond-Winchester Turnpike, where it could be seen by passing tourists. It now stands at the original fort site. (DWC.)

The Most Historical Spot in Kentucky.

Boone was charged with finding a suitable location for the Transylvania Company's settlement. He chose a site near the Kentucky River that had a freshwater spring and two sulfur springs. The springs were located in a small depression they called Sycamore Hollow from the large trees growing there. Sycamore trees still flourish in the hollow, which the photograph refers to as "The Most Historic Spot in Kentucky." (DWC.)

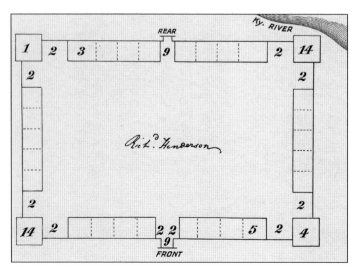

This plan of Fort Boonesborough was adapted from a sketch by Richard Henderson. Although work began in April 1775, the fort was not completed until just before the great siege in September 1778. The following points are identified: (1) Henderson's cabin, (2) stockading, (3) Henderson's kitchen, (4, 5) Luttrell's cabin and kitchen, (9) gates, and (14) Hart's and Williams' cabins. (AC.)

28

Stockaded forts like Boonesborough offered a high level of protection to pioneers from attacks by Native American Indians. Unless they had cannons, these fortifications proved nearly impossible to breach. Blockhouses were an important part of the fort's defensive system. They had overhanging second stories and loopholes—narrow slits in the logs—that provided a shooting port with a wide field of fire and presented the attacking enemy a very small target. The thick stockade walls were impervious to bullets and difficult to set on fire. However, these forts provided an unpleasant and unsanitary environment for those forced to live in them for months or years at a time. Fort Boonesborough had several additional weaknesses. Being so close to the river, it was subject to flooding, and it could be fired into from the surrounding hillsides. (Both, RAP.)

Before the locks and dams were built on the Kentucky River, there was a rocky shoal at the mouth of Lower Howard's Creek that allowed crossing the river in times of low flow. Blackfish Ford was named for the Shawnee Chief Blackfish, who led more than 400 warriors to attack Fort Boonesborough in September 1778. (AC.)

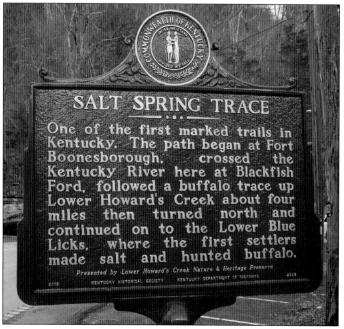

Boonesborough pioneers began using this trail to the Lower Blue Licks in 1775. From Fort Boonesborough, the trail crossed the Kentucky River at Blackfish Ford, proceeded up Lower Howard's Creek, and continued on to the Lower Blue Licks. Boone and a company of men from the fort were making salt at the lick when they were captured by a Shawnee war party led by Blackfish in 1778. (AC.)

This historic marker at Fort Boonesborough State Park commemorates the "Divine Elm," a magnificent tree once the focal point for many fort activities. Near the fort, Richard Henderson wrote, "Stands one of the finest Elms that perhaps nature ever produced in any region." He said it was four feet in diameter, and its crown spread one hundred feet. The tree fell to the woodsman's axe in 1828. (DWC.)

In June 1775, Boone went back to Virginia to retrieve his family. His return trip that September is depicted in a painting by George Caleb Bingham entitled *Daniel Boone Escorting Settlers through the Cumberland Gap*. Bingham used Biblical and classical imagery to depict their entry into "the promised land." Boone leads a white horse carrying Rebecca, here portrayed as a Madonna figure. (MLKAM.)

One Sunday afternoon in July 1776, Jemima Boone and Fannie and Betsy Callaway went canoeing on the Kentucky River. The girls drifted close to the bank opposite the fort and were taken by five Indians, shown here in a lithograph of Karl Bodmer's *Capture of the Daughters of D. Boone and Callaway by the Indians.* Two days later, a rescue party led by Boone overtook the Indians and recovered the girls safely. (MLKAM.)

The first marriage in Kentucky was celebrated at Fort Boonesborough on August 7, 1776, between Samuel Henderson and Elizabeth "Betsy" Callaway. The first reenactment of this event took place at the Sesqui-Centennial Pageant Celebration at Harrodsburg in 1924. After Fort Boonesborough State Park was established in 1965, a reenactment of the wedding became a regular event at the park. (DWC.)

In September 1778, an army of 400 Shawnees led by Chief Blackfish laid siege to Fort Boonesborough in an effort to drive the settlers out of Kentucky. When the fort could not be taken after 10 days, the Indians withdrew. The event is re-enacted every September at Fort Boonesborough State Park. (KC.)

Col. Richard Henderson called a meeting of representatives from the Kentucky settlements to meet at Boonesborough. The group, styled the Transylvania House of Delegates, convened in May 1775 and has been called Kentucky's first legislature. The three-day session, conducted under the Divine Elm, resulted in the passage of nine bills and the signing of a compact between the proprietors of the company and the people. (AC.)

Three of the great sycamore trees in Sycamore Hollow, present when Boonesborough was settled, survived into the late 19th century. One fell to the woodman's axe in 1873 and another in 1885. The ancient sycamore, pictured left in about 1915, was a magnet for tourists who climbed its branches and carved initials in the bark. The last of the sentinels, it was removed in 1932. (DWC.)

Nathaniel Hart, one of the three Harts of the Transylvania Company, settled on his own place a half mile from Fort Boonesborough that he called White Oak Spring Station. Hart was killed by Indians near Redhouse in 1782. The Hart family home on his land was often referred to as the oldest house in Madison County until it burned in the 1980s. (EKU.)

Kentucky Frontier

Scale in Miles
0   20   40   60

By 1784, Boonesborough residents had begun dismantling the old fort, and many left for other areas. This map of the frontier shows numerous settlements that had sprung up in central Kentucky in less than a decade after Boonesborough and Harrodsburg were established. Immigrants to Kentucky mainly came by one of two routes: down the Ohio River where they usually disembarked at Limestone or over Boone Trace through Cumberland Gap. The map shows Martins and Ruddles, the only two stations captured by Indians up to that time. When Daniel Boone returned to Kentucky from North Carolina in 1779, he established Boone's Station near present-day Athens (shown on the map as "Boone's"). Lower Blue Licks was where the pioneers went to hunt buffalo and make salt. Within a few years, the Kentucky and Ohio Rivers would become part of an important route for exporting goods and produce to markets in New Orleans. (NOH.)

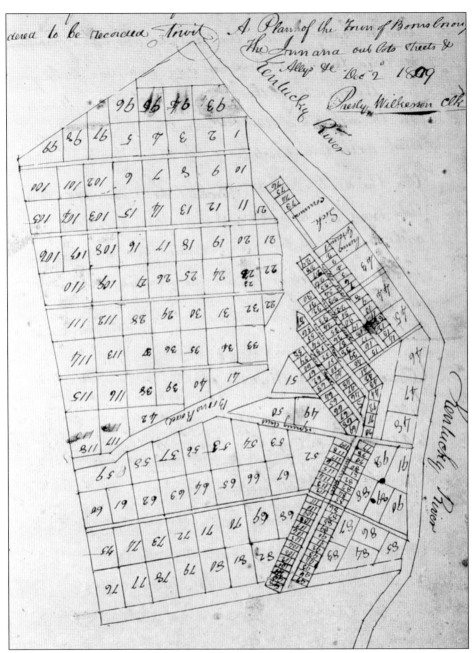

In 1779, the Virginia General Assembly established the "Town of Boonsborough," the first in Kentucky. After the fort broke up, a small community continued residing at Boonesborough. In 1792, a number of prominent landholders raised pledges totaling more than 20,000 pounds sterling in an effort to persuade the state to locate the capital at Boonesborough. (Frankfort was selected instead.) A plat of the town filed in 1809 shows in- and out-lots, and two areas designated as "Lick Commons" and "buring [sic] Ground." The streets include Water, Middle, Main, Back, and Spring, as well as Boone Road. The 1810 US census listed eight families living in Boonesborough, 68 persons in all. The town found it difficult to sell the in- and out-lots and then had trouble collecting payment from those who purchased on credit. (MCOB.)

36

John Halley (c. 1746–1838) came to Boonesborough in 1780. Halley built a gristmill, operated an inspection warehouse, and took at least two flatboat trips carrying produce to New Orleans. He received a license to keep a tavern in his house in 1818. His house was located in the present parking area across from the state park entrance. It was destroyed by lightning in the late 1960s. (WFC.)

Filson Club president R.T. Durrett once said, "Boonesborough, like a mist of the morning, has vanished." This photograph, taken in 1900, shows a cornfield on the site of Fort Boonesborough. Not a trace of the old fort remained. Continued site disturbance resulted in the exact fort location becoming a matter of dispute until an archaeological survey conducted by Nancy O'Malley in 1987 confirmed the location. (EKU.)

On May 25, 1840, the first Boonesborough celebration was held to honor the establishment of Kentucky's first settlement. Celebrities present included Keziah Callaway French and her enslaved servant Dolly, who had resided at the old fort; Gov. Charles Wickliffe; and former governors James T. Morehead (above) and Thomas Metcalf. Morehead's lengthy address has been reprinted many times. Later, it was proven that Harrodsburg was actually Kentucky's first settlement. (AC.)

Thomas H. Stevens, owner of the original site of Fort Boonesborough, donated a small tract of land—50 feet by 50 feet—to the Boonesborough Chapter of the DAR. In 1907, the group erected a monument honoring early Boonesborough settlers. The monument was placed on the exact spot where the old fort had stood. That location became the subject of intense debate until finally verified by archaeologists. (EKU.)

PROGRAMME

Unveiling of Monument at Fort Boonesborough

—BY—

Boonesborough Chapter, Daughters of the American Revolution

Saturday, October 5th, 1907

Invocation. . . . . **Rev. Hugh McLellan**

MUSIC BY THE WINCHESTER MILITARY BAND.

Address . . . .**Col. J. W. Caperton**

MUSIC.

Address . . . .**Hon. James B. McCreary**

MUSIC.

Address . . . .**Judge George B. Kinkead**

MUSIC.

Address . . . . **Judge J. M. Benton**

MUSIC.

Address . . . . **Hon. C. F. Burnam**

MUSIC.

UNVEILING MONUMENT.

Salute by Normal School Cadets, Commanded by Col. E. H. Crawford.

MUSIC.

Benediction . . . .**Rev. G. W. Shepherd**

LUNCHEON.

MUSIC.

Nearly 67 years after the Boonesborough celebration of 1840, hundreds of people from Madison, Clark, Bourbon, and other counties gathered at Boonesborough for the dedication of the Pioneer Monument. The monument was unveiled on October 5, 1907. One side of the stone was inscribed with "In memory of the Pioneers of Kentucky. Erected by the Boonesboro Chapter DAR." Some visitors arrived by train, disembarking at Ford, two miles upstream from Boonesborough, and then boarding a steamer for the trip downriver to the dedication. The Winchester Military Band played "My Old Kentucky Home," and the Richmond Normal School cadets fired a salute. Prominent local speakers then regaled the crowd, many of whom were descendants of the pioneers. After the formal ceremonies were completed, the crowd was treated to lunch on the grounds. (DWC.)

An American flag was raised at the Pioneer Monument dedication as the Winchester Military Band played "The Star-Spangled Banner." Col. James W. Caperton (pictured below), a Union veteran of the Civil War and Richmond attorney, gave the opening address and read the names listed on the monument. He was followed by US senator James B. McCreary, who had served as the 27th and 37th governor of Kentucky; Judge George B. Kinkead of Lexington; and Judge J. M. Benton of Winchester. The monument was unveiled by children of the Boonesborough Chapter of the DAR. The audience included many descendants of the honored pioneers. (Both, EKU.)

Kentucky was one of 25 states represented at the Jamestown Ter-Centennial Exposition held from April through November 1907 in Norfolk, Virginia. Kentucky's Exposition Commission decided that the state's exhibit at the World's Fair should be a reproduction of Fort Boonesborough. The fort was constructed in a pine grove that provided one of the few shaded venues at the Exposition. It measured 200 feet by 100 feet and had four two-story blockhouses at the corners that had protruding upper stories (above). The fort surround was a waist-high fence rather than log stockading. The Center House (below) had two 18-foot-square rooms, large fireplaces with oak slab mantels, exterior chimneys, wide porches, and a covered entryway. (Both, DWC.)

Kentucky's popular exhibit, with an estimated 100,000 visitors, was the only one open evenings and Sundays. On July 16, declared Kentucky Day, over 2,000 visitors were treated to an old-fashioned barbeque. The chefs spent several days preparing a traditional Kentucky burgoo in large cauldrons. On October 5, the fort hosted an all-day outing for a group of 150 orphans from Norfolk. (DWC.)

An unidentified group of men and women visited the Pioneer Monument in the summer of 1910. Some are standing on the monument, while others sit. All are fashionably dressed. A wire fence is visible in the background. This photograph was taken before the DAR built the stone fence surrounding the monument. (EKU.)

In 1935, the Transylvanians, a patriotic society, celebrated the bicentennial of Richard Henderson's birth. The founder of the Transylvania Company was honored at Boonesborough with the unveiling of a granite monument whose engraved bronze tablets memorialize four events: the founding of the Company in Hillsboro, North Carolina, cutting the Boone Trace to Kentucky, the first legislative session held at Boonesborough, and the first religious service held in Kentucky. (DWC.)

Dr. Jonathan T. Dorris, professor and historian at Eastern Kentucky University, had several gavels and other small carvings made from the last giant sycamore tree which stood in Sycamore Hollow outside the fort. The tree had died and was finally cut down in the early 1930s. Many of the gavels were given to judges and other politicians by Dr. Dorris. (DWC.)

An archaeological survey conducted by Nancy O'Malley identified a number of historic sites in the Boonesborough area in addition to the old fort. These included seven residences, two tobacco inspection warehouses, and a spring. Based on her publication, *Searching for Boonesborough* (published in 1989), the National Park Service designated Fort Boonesborough a National Historic Landmark (in 1996) exemplifying an outstanding aspect of American history and culture. (DWC.)

Friends of Boone Trace are working to rediscover, restore, and preserve the route Boone and his axemen blazed in 1775. Their vision is to create a multi-use trail closely approximating the original Boone Trace that can be traveled by motor vehicles, cyclists, or pedestrians. Friends president Dr. John Fox stands beneath one of the Daniel Boone Bike Route signs that will eventually grace US Bicycle Route 21. (JF.)

Three

Boonesborough Ferry and Bridge

Boonesborough Ferry was the first in Kentucky. By an act of October 30, 1779, the Virginia General Assembly assigned rights to operate the ferry to Col. Richard Callaway, who was a member of the legislature. Callaway was killed by Indians on March 8, 1780, while working on his ferry boat. The ferry ran until a bridge was built across the Kentucky River at Boonesborough in 1931. (DWC.)

This 1907 view is one of the oldest photographs of the Boonesborough Ferry that operated under a series of proprietors from 1779 until 1931. The earliest-known ferry operator was John Sidebottom, an African American Revolutionary War veteran, whose tenancy under William Bush and Robert Clark dates to 1791. Later owners include the Stevens family, George Bentley, and Dr. David J. Williams. (EKU.)

This is another early view of the Boonesborough Ferry with a wagon and team preparing to board. The cable ferry, which did not have a source of mechanical power, was guided across the river by a cable attached to either bank. The ferry transported people, livestock, wagons, and later, cars across the Kentucky River. Three other boats stand near the Clark County ferry landing, a canoe, and two scows. (DWC.)

This undated photograph of the wooden ferry boat docked at Boonesborough has a caption identifying Carlos Sharp (left) and Will Asher. Asher was the operator of the Boonesborough ferry in the 1920s. A sternwheel diesel towboat near the Clark County ferry landing may have been the pilot boat for the ferry. (WFC.)

The Boonesborough car ferry is shown departing for the Clark County landing. From the time it was established in 1779 until a bridge over the Kentucky River was erected in 1931, the ferry was an essential link on the main road from Winchester to Richmond. Madison and Clark County citizens petitioned the legislature for years before they appropriated funds to build the bridge. (DWC.)

In 1928, the Kentucky Highway Department began planning for a new bridge to carry traffic across the Kentucky River on the federal highway from Winchester to Richmond. In October 1929, the War Department approved Kentucky's application for a permit to construct the bridge. The Commonwealth of Kentucky purchased the right-of-way for the bridge from David J. Williams, who was still operating the ferry at the time. Contracts for bridge construction were signed in October 1930. Successful bidders were J.A. Kreis & Sons, Inc. of Knoxville, Tennessee, for the concrete substructure ($119,360) and Vincennes Bridge Co. of Vincennes, Indiana, for the steel superstructure ($56,337). Work was to be completed within one year. Three steel spans, weighing 3,600 tons each, were raised onto the concrete piers by huge derricks in May 1931. (Both, WFC.)

DANIEL BOONE MEMORIAL BRIDGE, KENTUCKY RIVER
McDAUGHEY STUDIO · RICHMOND, KY·

The Fort Boonesborough Memorial Bridge (misnamed "Daniel Boone Memorial Bridge" by the photography studio) was dedicated on Armistice Day 1931. A crowd of 2,000 attended the ceremonies in spite of the rain. The 961-foot iron-truss span opened as a toll bridge charging a base rate of 45¢ until the bonds were paid off. The toll was reduced to 30¢ in 1938 and eliminated in 1945. (EKU.)

The statue of Daniel Boone overlooking the bridge on the Clark County side of the river was funded by $1,200 in donations and created by A.D. Fisher, owner of Fisher Monument Company in Winchester. The eight-foot-tall statue carved from a five-ton block of Bedford stone stood on a 12-foot pedestal. After the unveiling in 1933, some critics opined that the statue more resembled Fisher than Daniel Boone. (DWC.)

In 1931, the Boonesborough Chapter of the DAR presented the state with a bronze tablet commemorating Fort Boonesborough that was installed on a marble monument (above) at the Boonesborough bridge approach in Madison County. The plaque inscription paid tribute to the pioneers who settled Boonesborough in 1775 and withstood sieges by the Indians in 1777 and 1778. However, the statement that "Fort Boonesborough was the First Fort to be Built in Kentucky" was challenged by Harrodsburg, which is now acknowledged as the first settlement and fort. The tablet was later removed and attached to the stone fence surrounding the Pioneer Monument at Fort Boonesborough State Park (below). At some point, vandals stole the tablet, and its present whereabouts are unknown. (Left, DWC; below, WSPC.)

The new bridge was intended to replace the Boonesborough ferry that had connected Clark and Madison Counties for 152 years. As seen above, the ferry continued to run for a time after the new bridge opened. The ferry owner, David Williams, kept the business going to serve those who protested having to pay for crossing the toll bridge. (EKU.)

When the new road from Winchester to Richmond (KY 627) was completed in 1976, the old bridge proved hazardous for modern vehicles, especially tractor-trailers. Due to its narrow width and curved approaches, the heavily traveled bridge was the scene of many accidents. This 1992 view shows a massive pier under construction at the edge of the river with a smaller approach pier in the background. (WSPC.)

The state replaced the old 1931 bridge with a new $6.6 million span. Here, a platform-mounted crane has raised steel spans onto piers from both sides of the river prior to installing the center spans in place. The new KY 627 bridge opened for traffic in 1994. (EKU.)

This aerial view of the new bridge shows Ford Road branching off (far left), and Waterfront Restaurant (bottom) stands near the river. Allen Company's Boonesborough Quarry occupies both sides of the road on the Madison side. The state park campground begins just to the left of the quarry. The park extends up to the lock and dam, which can be seen in the upper-left corner. (WH.)

Four

Kentucky River Lock and Dam 10

Between 1883 and 1917, the US Army Corps of Engineers built 14 locks and dams on the Kentucky River to provide reliable year-round navigation along its 255-mile course. This rare photograph of Lock 10 under construction at Boonesborough shows workers testing the steel lock gates. After the Corps abandoned the stone masonry-timber crib method, this was one of the first Kentucky River locks and dams built of concrete and steel. (COE.)

Loose logs, like these shown near Ford, caused a disaster at the nearly completed dam at Boonesborough. In March 1905, the frozen river thawed and 300,000 logs went tearing downstream. The logs, piled 20 feet high, crashed into the dam and scoured out a new 240-foot-wide channel on the Madison County side, leaving the lock in the middle of the river. (MF.)

This photograph, taken from the Clark County shore, shows the original dam (left) and auxiliary dam (right) that was built at a cost of $100,000 after the flanking disaster in 1905. That event also uncovered a fine sand beach (far right) that would become a major Boonesborough attraction for years to come. (COE.)

The Walters family lived and worked at Lock 10 from 1906 when John Sr. started until 1975 when John Jr. retired. They served as lockmasters for most of those years. Family members pictured from left to right are John A. Walters Sr., wife Mabel, and children Ann, Ethel, Martha "Mot," Emma, Ruby, Dorothy, Alice, John A. Jr. ("Jay"), Mary, and Wilma ("Puss"). When together like this, they joked that it was "the whole dam family." (WFP.)

Oswald Hood "Hink" Harney and Martha "Mot" Walters pose with his touring car beside the Boonesboro Beach Resort hotel. Hink was a grandson of John Bell Hood, a Confederate general in the Civil War. He came from a wealthy family in Lexington. The couple married in 1923. (WFP.)

The Walters family and their friends spent a lot of time at the beach. Jenimarie Sowers, a granddaughter of John Walters Sr., recalled that almost every weekend Walters family members would get together on the reservation. Many of her cousins spent their entire summer vacations down by the river. Jenimarie recalled, "Gatherings at the lock were like a big family reunion. There would be singing, dancing, swimming, and fishing, and the children would play games, including checkers, cards, and hopscotch. The women would prepare an absolute feast with everything from ham and fried chicken to mashed potatoes, green beans, and homemade biscuits. It was not all fun and games though. During their stay on the reservation, the older cousins were expected to help out with household chores. They would sweep the stairs and the porch, dust the house, help with the dishes, and hang the laundry outside to dry." During these family gatherings, the lockmaster and lockman were still responsible for the operation of the lock. When they were not locking through boats, they did maintenance work on the lock and dam reservation. (WFP.)

The lockmaster's house and one for his assistant stood on the Madison side of the river, on the hill overlooking the dam. Structures on the Corps reservations were well-built according to a standard set of plans. The lockhouses, outbuildings, and grounds had to be well maintained, and the lock had to be kept in good working order. (WFP.)

This view of the reservation from the 1920s or 1930s shows one of the government skiffs tied up to the shore. The lock could not be reached from shore via the auxiliary dam (shown starting at the right and running to the abutment on the shore). Lockmasters had to row out to the lock to operate the gates. An office (shown on the dike) was built to provide access to the lock during high water. (WFP.)

A group of visitors stand on the dam abutment at the Clark County shore. This 1915 photograph provides a good view of the original dam, lock, auxiliary dam, and Corps reservation. Water pours over the original dam during high water but not the auxiliary dam, which was built 10 feet higher. (EKU.)

The steamboat *Gregory* with living quarter barges is shown entering Lock 10 heading upstream (date unknown). The Clark County shore is in the background directly across from the beach at Fort Boonesborough State Park. The Corps of Engineers maintenance crews would stay for a few days to a few weeks depending on needed repairs. (WFC.)

Every year, the US Army Corps of Engineers fleet quartered at Frankfort came up the river to repair the lock. One boat in the fleet would have a crane to lift the lock gates out of the water for repairs, and another boat would have a dredge for clearing the river of obstructions and excess sediment. Corps officials also performed regular inspections of the lock and dam as well as the reservation. Major problems tended to be eroding concrete lock walls and rusting steel lock gates. Lock gates closed in a V-shape with the point of the V facing upstream, which provided stability to resist the river's current pushing against the gates. The massive lock gates (below) dwarf laborers at work on the gates. (Both, WFP.)

Thomas Walters is shown locking small boats through Lock 10 in October 1981, on the last day before the lock closed for the season. By that time, pleasure craft occupied most of the lockmasters' workload, as commercial traffic on the river had essentially ceased. Beginning in 1975, the locks did not operate during the winter months. (WFP.)

Charlie Warner and Anne Johnson are shown on their boat in Lock 10 in this 1970s photograph. The Corps of Engineers decommissioned Locks 5–14 in 1990, and the Kentucky River Authority (KRA) operated the locks through 1994. The Corps deeded Lock 10 to the state in 1996. The KRA began a program of permanently closing locks 5–14 and upgrading dams that impound public water supplies. Upgrade of the Boonesborough lock and dam was completed in 2021. (WFP.)

Five

BOONESBORO BEACH RESORT

Dr. David J. Williams (1872–1923), a native of Wales, came to America in 1893 and practiced medicine at Ford in Clark County and later at Redhouse in Madison County. In 1898, he began buying land along Otter Creek and Kentucky River, and by 1920, he was the major landowner in the Boonesborough area. (WFC.)

When Dr. Williams moved to Madison County, he lived in this house located between Boonesborough and Redhouse, near the Boonesborough railroad station. In 1907, the DAR erected a monument to the pioneers at Fort Boonesborough. Several years later, Dr. Williams capitalized on the renewed interest in the old fort and the growing tourism industry along the river to build a resort near Boonesborough Beach. (WFC.)

Shearer Station (building at the left) on the Louisville & Nashville Railroad (L&N) was located two miles south of Boonesborough. After Dr. Williams began constructing his resort, he convinced the railroad to change the name to Boonesborough Station. The resort offered car service to and from the station. A water tower for steam locomotives can be seen at the far right. (WFC.)

In 1913, Williams acquired the historic Boonesborough ferry from George Bentley, who had run it for many years. As seen above, the ferry at that time was a crude unmotorized wooden raft that was guided across the river by a cable. Williams modernized the operation with steel ferry boats and sternwheel pilot boats. The ferry remained in business until shortly after the bridge was built across the Kentucky River in 1931. In the 1920s scene below, four well-dressed passengers and their Model T Ford are shown heading for the landing on the Madison County side of the river. The *Daniel Boone*, a flat-bottom, gasoline-powered sternwheeler, guided the ferry. (Both, WFC.)

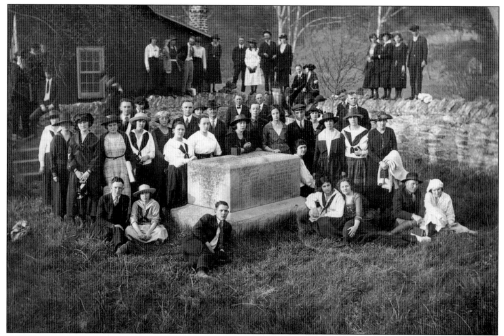

Dr. Williams acquired the site of the old fort from Thomas H. Stevens in 1909 and announced plans to build a hotel and operate a summer destination he called "Boonesboro Beach Resort." The main attraction was Boonesborough Beach, but many day visitors came to view the DAR's Pioneer Monument. One of Williams' resort cabins can be seen at the left rear of this 1915 photograph. (EKU.)

The resort became a popular site for class trips. Prof. George "Bug" Smith, who came to Eastern Kentucky State Normal School (now Eastern Kentucky University) in 1908, enjoyed leading students on field trips. This oversized excursion boat near the Boonesborough ferry landing shows Smith's class on a visit in 1915. Most of those on board are women, as Eastern at that time was a teaching college. (EKU.)

Williams constructed a row of frame "camp cabins" near the beach for overnight guests. Local news stories often referred to the guests as "camping at Boonesborough." Each cabin had two bedrooms, a kitchen, and a bathroom. There would eventually be 10 of these built. Williams laid his own water line to supply the cabins. In 1920, he installed an electric light plant at the resort to supply the hotel and cabins. (WFC.)

At first, the beach was the main attraction at the Boonesboro Beach Resort. Dr. Williams installed a diving platform at the beach. Picnics on the beach celebrated special occasions, boats were available to rent and moonlight cruises were held. As seen here, two of the guests in this group at their camp cabin are outfitted in swimming attire. Dr. Williams soon added other attractions at the resort, and it became a go-to spot in Central Kentucky. (WFC.)

During the summer season of 1919, Williams heavily advertised the Boonesboro Beach Resort. He touted cottages for rent by the day, week, or month; a dining hall; 500 dressing rooms with individual lockers and bathing suits to rent; and the three-fourths-mile-long beach, "the finest in the State of Kentucky." The photograph above shows the dance hall (left of center) and the bathhouses (on the right, topped by an American flag). The hotel would be built at the extreme left, just out of the picture. The photograph below shows a row of rental cabins to the right of the bathhouses. The popular diving barge can be seen near the beach. (Both, WFC.)

This photograph shows another pre-hotel era event at Boonesborough Beach. From the American flags and patriotic bunting, it appears to be a Fourth of July celebration and has drawn a sizeable crowd. The stage, visible on the right, was used for speeches by dignitaries and other forms of entertainment. (WFC.)

This photograph is from the same event described at top, with the same decorated stage. There is a sternwheel towboat docked at the beach (left of center). Since no one in the crowd is wearing bathing suits, it appears that most visitors were there for the Fourth of July celebration. The four doughboys in the foreground may date the photograph to 1919 or 1920. (WFC.)

In July 1921 the *Lexington Herald-Leader* reported that "Dr. D. J. Williams has a force of carpenters at work constructing a large hotel at Boonesboro Beach on the Madison county side of the river." It was located in what is now the maintenance yard of the state park. The hotel featured 15 guest rooms, a large dining hall, and "all the modern conveniences," namely, heat and water. (WFC.)

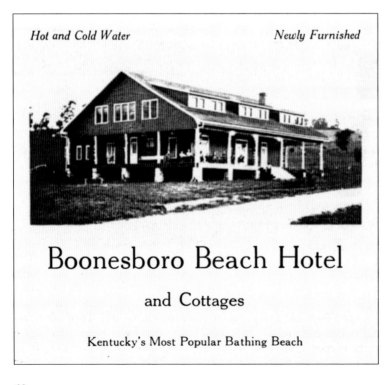

Hot and Cold Water   Newly Furnished

Boonesboro Beach Hotel

and Cottages

Kentucky's Most Popular Bathing Beach

The hotel held its grand opening on June 8, 1922. They touted "unexcelled cuisine" and "meals at all hours," as well as the black and white sulfur springs, and lithia and chalybeate mineral waters. For the opening, there was a special moonlight cruise on the Kentucky River on the pleasure barge *Amta*. (WFC.)

The main drawing card, however, was a dance at the new Merry Garden, featuring Johnson and Gray's Society Orchestra, the "Seven Apostles of Pop." That summer the Merry Garden Dancing Pavilion, shown with the welcome sign over the entrance, held dances every night except Mondays ("instruction night"). The hotel manager was R.C. White, and the Merry Garden was managed by Johnson and Gray. (WFC.)

The Richmond American Legion Post held a picnic at the resort on July 4, 1922. The day's events included boxing, wrestling, swimming, and diving matches, a concert by the American Legion Band, and as indicated in the photograph, a Ford Touring Car was given away "absolutely free." The Merry Garden was open for dancing from noon to 3:00 a.m. (WFC.)

Special events at the resort drew enormous crowds. The examples shown here, possibly from the July 4th American Legion picnic in 1922, show a throng of people converging on the beach (above) while others gather in front of a concession tent (below). A July 1917 newspaper caption announced, "Five Thousand Bathers at Boonesboro Beach," and went on to state that it was a record-breaker for attendance at the bathing beach. The article reported there were over 1,000 people bathing at one time during the afternoon. They concluded that "Boonesboro is fast becoming one of the most famous bathing resorts in the State." (Both, WFC.)

The Winchester American Legion Post held a Labor Day picnic at the resort on September 4, 1922. They advertised boxing, wrestling and diving contests, dancing, fireworks, and "other amusements." Admission was 25¢. In this scene, dozens of automobiles obscure the large crowd gathered to watch the baseball game, a five-inning match between the Winchester Rotary and Kiwanis Clubs and the Richmond Rotary and Exchange Clubs. The watermelon wagon in the center foreground seems out of place in the presence of so many "modern" conveyances. Several rental cottages can be seen in the background. The photograph was taken from a second-floor window at the hotel. (WFC.)

After getting his resort firmly established, Dr. Williams passed away in the fall of 1923. His son David J. Williams Jr. took over management. He continued to introduce novelties to attract visitors, such as this miniature steam excursion train that ran between the cottages, dance hall, and hotel. In addition to the beach, other attractions included tennis courts, horseback riding, a baseball field, and frequent fireworks displays. (WFC.)

This 1930s photograph shows the "foot ferry" that transported pedestrians from Clark County straight over to the beach and was a separate business from the vehicle ferry operating downstream. Also called a "hand ferry," since the riders had to pull the boat across the river by hand via a rope attached to each bank. It operated until World War II, carrying passengers to the privately owned Boonesboro Beach Resort. (EKU.)

Barge parties were a fashionable form of entertainment in the 1920s and 1930s. The events featured swimming in the river, picnics on the beach, and sometimes a tow down the river sightseeing. Newspaper accounts list dozens of these swimming parties held at Boonesborough Beach by professional organizations, fraternal societies, and women's clubs. This undated photograph, labeled "Tommy K at Boonesborough beach," belongs to the latter group. (DWC.)

The resort hotel lobby had a number of props available for patron photographs. One of the most popular was the bucking bronco ride. In the late 1930s, young Fannie Lee Howard (1924–1991), a Madison County native, had her picture taken on the "wild horse." Fannie married Dean Whitaker of Richmond. Both are buried in Richmond Cemetery. (DWC.)

Williams had two pilot boats constructed to conduct the ferry more quickly and safely across the river. The *Boonesboro*, shown here, is preparing to leave the Clark County landing. It was built in 1926 and measured 33 feet long. The other, named the *Daniel Boone*, 26 feet long, was built in 1919. The ferry itself was a 91-foot-long steel barge built in 1926. (WFC.)

Madison was a dry county, and it was said that the lack of liquor sales eventually did in the resort. Over the years, the facilities deteriorated. By the time the state moved in to buy the property for Fort Boonesborough State Park in the 1960s, the hotel was still in fair condition but the dance hall had collapsed, the bathhouses were in poor shape, and only two cabins remained barely habitable. (WFC.)

Six

FORT BOONESBOROUGH STATE PARK

After the Boonesboro Beach Resort closed, David Williams Jr. sold 57 acres to the Kentucky Department of Parks in 1963 to establish Fort Boonesborough State Park. The park was dedicated in October 1965. The beach, shown here in the spring of 1970, continued to be a popular attraction for swimming and sunbathing. Boats traveling up or down the river could dock at the beach. (WSPC.)

When the park opened in 1965, the campground was located in the Sycamore Hollow area with 50 campsites. During the park makeover in 1974, the campground was expanded to 166 sites. A new area for recreational vehicles was laid out north of Sycamore Hollow, while the latter area was set aside for primitive camping. (WSPC.)

The state built a bathhouse at the park in the summer of 1968 to accommodate swimmers. The $450,000 project featured a bathhouse, restrooms, and snack bar on the lower level and a 10,000-square-foot restaurant on the upper level. The restaurant closed after several years due to lack of business, which was blamed on the absence of liquor sales. (WSPC.)

In November 1971, at a luncheon at the state park, Gov. Louie Nunn announced plans to construct an authentic replica of the original Fort Boonesborough. Some $1.7 million was allocated for the fort and for new camping and picnic areas and a boat dock. Shown here with Robert Collins, president of the Clark County Historical Society, Nunn played an important role in the expansion of Kentucky's state park system. (WSPC.)

The 35-man professional construction crew began work on the new fort in September 1973. The crews worked on this test cabin in order to learn how to erect plumb walls using logs of different diameters and not entirely straight. The cabins were built on concrete foundations which were then covered with packed dirt to simulate pioneer conditions. (WSPC.)

Lane Hargett Construction of Lexington was awarded a $1.6 million contract to build the replica fort. The project called for 10,000 logs to be shipped in from Alabama. Workers tapered the ends to resemble hand-hewn logs. Builders erected 26 cabins, 4 blockhouses, a blacksmith shop, and a powder magazine on a hilltop about half a mile from the original fort site. The fort measures 301 feet long by 203 feet wide, slightly larger than the original. Fireplaces and chimneys are native Kentucky limestone from Scott County. Most of the fireplaces house heating and air conditioning units. The huge laminated beams in the blockhouses came from North Carolina. Roofs have two layers of shakes, or wooden shingles, from California. Most nails and bolts were hidden, as were electrical and plumbing lines. (Both, WSPC.)

In the summer of 1974, construction of the replica fort nears completion at Fort Boonesborough State Park. The new fort was sited on a plateau above the original fort location to avoid being damaged by periodic flooding of the Kentucky River. The gate shown on the right side is to serve as the main entrance. In the center stands the blacksmith's shop with a lean-to roof and powder magazine bunker. (WSPC.)

The expanded campground allowed recreational vehicles, shown here in Sycamore Hollow, to move to new spaces with water and electrical hookups. Sycamore Hollow was set aside for tent campers. In addition to growing to about 165 acres, park improvements featured complete new water, electric, and sewage systems; new roads; a boat dock and launching ramp; beach improvements; and landscaping. (WSPC.)

A new amenity at the state park was a modern boat dock located near the boat launching ramp. The dock allowed park visitors to arrive by way of the river. The dock had a gas pump, snack bar, and paddleboats for rent. Like many other Kentucky River docks, this one eventually succumbed to a spring flood. (WSPC.)

A giant slide, shown here under construction in 1974, offered a thrilling ride to park visitors. It was located near the present picnic shelter. The popular attraction was removed over safety concerns a few years after it opened when several youths were injured on the slide in an after-hours incident. (WSPC.)

A new entrance to the state park was part of the $2 million park upgrade in 1974. The park was expected to triple the number of visitors after the new fort opened and all park renovations were completed. Although open only for two months, over 60,000 people toured the new fort during the 1974 season. Admission cost $2 for adults and $1 for children. (WSPC.)

The southeast blockhouse at the replica fort shows construction typical for these defensive structures. The two-story log building has an overlapping upper floor with "loopholes" that allowed its defenders to fire in various directions. Fort Boonesborough had one at each of its four corners. They played a major role in repelling the siege by the Shawnee Indians in September 1778. (WSPC.)

On opening day, August 30, 1974, the first guests officially admitted to the new fort were Gov. Wendell Ford and his wife, Jean. Jouette "Bucky" Walters, shown at the right holding the log gate open, was the first fort manager. At that time, there was no parking at the fort. Visitors rode a gas-powered tram up the steep hill from the parking lot below. (WSPC.)

Gov. Wendell Ford gave the dedication address at the official opening of the fort. He said the fort would give visitors a chance to "walk back in history" and would be a welcome addition to the state's $700 million tourism industry. He touted it as a "working fort" with Kentuckians in pioneer dress offering craft demonstrations in the authentically furnished log cabins. (WSPC.)

Gov. Wendell Ford unveiled a dedication marker commemorating Fort Boonesborough and the Transylvania Company organized by Col. Richard Henderson of North Carolina and Daniel Boone who was hired to lead the expedition to Kentucky in 1775. The fort, built according to Henderson's plans, withstood two Indian attacks in 1777 and one in 1778. (WSPC.)

Several local organizations issued commissions to well-known artists to prepare paintings telling the story of Kentucky's settlement period. Jack Hodgkin of Winchester headed the committee that selected the artists. Russell May (second from the left) is shown here with his painting, "Boone Bringing Settlers through the Cumberland Gap," which hangs today in the orientation cabin. Pictured are Ewart Johnson, May, Gov. Wendell Ford, and Frank Downing. (WSPC.)

Paintings depicting pioneer times were to be installed in the art museum at the new fort. These included the works of Holly VanMeter of Winchester (above) shown with her portraits "Pioneer Women," and Nellie Meadows of Clay City (below) presenting fort manager Bucky Walters with her painting *Wildflowers of Boonesborough Settlement*, displaying one of Kentucky's native plants, jack-in-the-pulpit, *Arisaema triphyllum*. Other commissioned Kentucky artworks included Jack May's *Old Stone Church*, Robert A. Powell's *Boone and the Saltmakers*, Toss Chandler's *The First Wedding*, Kate Pendleton's *Inside the Cabin*, and a life-size portrait of Daniel Boone by Jack Hodgkin. (Both, WSPC.)

The southwest blockhouse served as the orientation stop for visitors, who were shown a 15-minute film about Daniel Boone and the settling of Boonesborough. From there, visitors could stop in at the blacksmith's shop in the center of the stockade and cabins dedicated to spinning and vegetable dyeing, weaving and quilting, cabinetry and woodcarving, pottery, seat caning and basketry, soap making, candle making, and dollmaking. (WSPC.)

Lily Newman (left) of Richmond and Martha Eubank of Winchester were doll makers at the fort specializing in corn husk dolls and stuffed dolls, respectively. "Grandma Eubank," as her name tag read, came to the fort at age 75 with a lifelong experience making dolls. Newman, a Letcher County native, later served as the fort manager. (WSPC.)

Alice Roe of Winchester demonstrates hand quilting in the weaving-quilting cabin. The former teacher and elementary school principal learned quilting after retiring. She studied with a quilting group at a local church until she felt confident enough to go out on her own. Her quilts took several months to complete. (WSPC.)

Neil Colmer is pictured dipping candles in the candle shop. On the shelf behind him are bottles containing fragrant oils used to make scented candles. A Berea College graduate, Colmer worked at Boonesborough for several years helping to set up the craft demonstration program. He became a full-time weaver, working his looms for 50 years until retiring. Colmer and his wife, Mary, operate Weaver's Bottom Craft Studio in Berea. (WSPC.)

Molly Stotts of Winchester demonstrates the art of cornshuck dollmaking. The dolls were made out of the dried leaves, or "husk," of a corn cob. Corn shuck dolls were made by Native Americans for more than a thousand years, and the craft was adopted by European settlers. Frontier craftspersons made homemade dolls for children. (WSPC.)

Spinner Sandra Wallin (left) and Janet Phillips stir up kettles of vegetable dyes to color the wool yarn they spin. Native plants were used to make the dye baths and lend natural earth-tone colors to the yarn, which the weavers, in turn, made into various articles. Her husband, Jerry Wallin, was the fort's first blacksmith. (WSPC.)

Minnie Yancey (left) stirs a kettle of melted lard, while apprentice Laura Huber (below) separates half-pound cakes of soap from each other with a kitchen knife. The soap had to be cured for 10 days before being put in the shop for sale. Yancey, a Berea resident, was the master soap maker at the fort, and Huber was a Lexington high school student who was just learning the craft. The soap recipe called for 5 pounds of fat and 13 ounces of lye in a half gallon of water. Store-bought lard was melted in a cast iron kettle over a slow fire. A lard-lye-water mixture was heated and then poured into a cloth-lined wooden tray to cool and solidify. (Both, WSPC.)

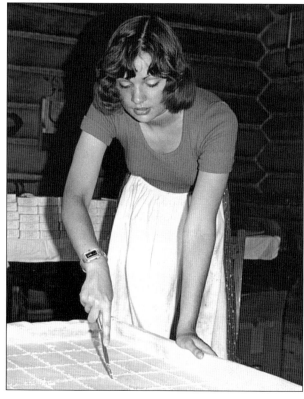

Kyle Whitaker of Winchester demonstrates his woodcraft for visitors while working at his period-authentic shaving horse. He was one of the carpenters at the fort and later worked at LexisNexis in Dayton, Ohio. He was also a talented chair caner, farmer, and gardener. In spite of going blind, Whitaker remained an avid woodworker all his life. (WSPC.)

Berea native Pat Gailey was the broom maker at the fort. Here she binds straw with twine to make a fan broom for sale in the fort gift shop. In addition to the fan broom, she also made long-handle brooms and straight whisk brooms. Each broom took 10 to 30 minutes to complete, depending on the style. (WSPC.)

Eli Johnson, basket maker and caner at the fort, rives a piece of white oak into splits to weave into one of his finely crafted baskets. Johnson selected his own wood from six- to eight-inch diameter oak trees, quartered it with a wooden mallet and froe, then used a knife and his fingers to separate the wood along the grain into very thin oak splits. (WSPC.)

Nesa McGee, a University of Kentucky philosophy major, was the weaver at the new fort. She is shown in the process of passing the shuttle beneath warp threads on a four-harness loom as she begins weaving a cotton wool coverlet. Her wool was dyed and spun at the fort. A coverlet took about a month to complete on the 75-year-old loom. (WSPC.)

Sue Cammarata and Jim Phillips, the Boonesborough potters, load the fort's kiln. The pair helped build the double-chambered, 11-inch-thick brick oven, where they fired and glazed the pots they threw. Very little has changed in the ancient art of throwing pots—clay plus a little water is still shaped by hand on a potter's wheel, dried, then kiln-fired. (WSPC.)

Sammy Meeks works on a bench leg using an antique treadle lathe from the 1770s. Meeks, the master craftsman in the woodworking shop, specialized in making benches and footstools and also built drop-leaf tables and other large pieces of furniture. He helped clean and set up the antique loom at the fort. (WSPC.)

C.G. Hayes, a Berea College graduate from North Carolina, was a woodcarver at the fort. He is shown carving a bushy-tailed squirrel. Many of his small figurines were whittled out of basswood, cedar, or buckeye with a sharp pocket knife. He built a cherry and red oak spinning wheel for the fort. In his spare time, Hayes made musical instruments, mostly dulcimers and banjos. (WSPC.)

Leigh Jones, from Monterey, California, checks the yarn spun onto a bobbin as she demonstrates the pioneer craft in the spinning cabin at the fort. The 200-year-old wheel is called a "walking wheel" because the spinner walks to and fro, turning clumps of carded wool into yarn to be dyed and woven into cloth. (WSPC.)

Louisville native Jerry Wallin was the master blacksmith as well as an award-winning metalsmith. He was hired to set up the forge at the fort. After Fort Boonesborough, Wallin and his wife, Mary, moved to Switzerland County, Indiana, where he took up woodworking. He specialized in making finely crafted Windsor chairs out of oak, hickory, and hard maple. (WSPC.)

Ike Berryman of Winchester demonstrates one of his "Limber Jacks" for an audience at the fort. Berryman made these wooden toys, also called "dancing dolls," that swing their legs and tap their toes on a flexible board balanced and tapped one's knee. These homemade toys were once common in Appalachian homes. (WSPC.)

Four days after the fort dedication, a small fire broke out in one of the blockhouses. The smoldering fire, probably caused by a carelessly discarded cigarette, resulted in extensive water and smoke damage to the gift shop. Park manager Otis Christian was overcome by smoke trying to extinguish the blaze and had to be hospitalized. (WSPC.)

The Boonesborough Bicentennial celebration began on April 1, 1975, the 200th anniversary of Daniel Boone's arrival at the fort site. A log cabin-topped birthday cake was cut by members of the commission, from left to right, Frank Downing, Clark County judge Dorsey Curtis, Winchester mayor Charles G. Stephenson, parks commissioner Ewart Johnson, Richmond mayor Wallace G. Maffett, commission president James Shannon, and Berea mayor Clint C. Hensley. (WSPC.)

Music for the Boonesborough Bicentennial celebration was provided by buckskin-clad musicians, including "Fiddlin' Dick" Wilson from Warsaw (center). A legendary performer from Wolfe County, Richard Wilson (1929–1998) collected and restored antique fiddles, rifles, and buggies. He also played the banjo and sang as exuberantly as he played. During the ceremonies, a new Kentucky Historical Marker for Fort Boonesborough was unveiled, and the new fort flag was raised at the fort entrance. The Kentucky Long Rifle Club fired several volleys in salute as dignitaries looked on. (Both, WSPC.)

On May 9, 1975, the Daniel Boone Walkers arrived at the fort, capping their 384-mile journey from Wilkes County, North Carolina, in a reenactment of Boone's 1775 trip. Hike leader Ivey Moore, 73 (pictured left foreground), was accompanied by Ralph L. Hooker, 70 (far right); Arthur Lain, 18; Charles Burke, 28; Ivey Moore, 14, a cousin of the leader; and Cherokee tribal chief Russell Sage Carter. (WSPC.)

A highlight of the 1975 Fort Boonesborough bicentennial festivities came on July 25, when Pat Boone and his family entertained a crowd of 25,000. Shown performing on the stage at Fort Boonesborough State Park from left to right are Cherry, 21; Lindy, 19; wife Shirley; Pat; Debby, 18; and Laury, 17. They had been performing together for several years as the Pat Boone Family. (WSPC.)

The relocated Boonesboro Road (KY 627) officially opened to traffic after the ribbon cutting on August 17, 1976, by Gov. Julian Carroll (with scissors) and other dignitaries. More than two years in the building, the $4 million, 5.8-mile highway replaced the old winding road from Winchester to the Kentucky River (KY 227). The new road carries traffic from Interstate 64 to Fort Boonesborough State Park. (WSPC.)

Boonesborough Beach lifeguards practice their CPR skills. The girls are wearing bathing suits designed to commemorate the 1976 Bicentennial. The state park held special events throughout the year. With the beach, reconstructed fort, and special events as attractions, Boonesborough set a new park attendance record in 1976. (WSPC.)

Centennial was a 12-episode television miniseries, based on the novel of the same name by James Michener, that aired on NBC from October 1978 to February 1979. The award-winning show was shot at multiple locations, including Fort Boonesborough State Park. Director Virgil Vogel sits in the director's chair inside the reconstructed fort while filming a sequence depicting a cannonade. (WSPC.)

Centennial, one of the longest and most ambitious television projects ever attempted up until that time, featured a cast of more than 30 distinguished actors. Major players included, from left to right, Barbara Carrera (Clay Basket) with her two boys, followed by Robert Conrad (Pasquinel), and Richard Chamberlain (Alexander McKeag). The action for the second episode filmed at Boonesborough was supposed to depict a fort located near St. Louis. (WSPC.)

TV actor Dallas McKennon made several trips to the state park. McKennon was a regular on the *Daniel Boone* television series (1964–1970). He played Cincinnatus, the tavern and storekeeper and a fixture of Boonesborough village life, usually appearing in his characteristic leather vest. McKennon was an American film, television, and voice actor who had a career lasting over 50 years. (WSPC.)

The Society of Boonesborough is a nonprofit group whose purpose is to collect and preserve a record of the pioneers who established Fort Boonesborough. In 1981, the society installed the Pioneer Ancestor Monument near the front gate of the replica fort. The five-foot-square granite marker with the engraved names of Boonesborough settlers was later topped with a 12-foot obelisk. (DWC.)

This aerial view shows Boonesborough Beach and bathhouse in the summer of 1969. The beach remained a popular attraction until the summer drought of 1988. Water-quality measurements showed that the river water had unacceptably high levels of bacteria, and the beach was closed to swimming. Water quality has much improved in recent years, but the swimming ban has never been lifted. (EKU.)

After the beach was closed for swimming for three straight years (1988–1990), the state approved plans to build a swimming pool at the park. The $1.2 million junior Olympic-size pool that opened in the summer of 1993 featured a 141-foot water slide, wading pool, misting fountain, concession stand, and restrooms. The facility stayed busy until it closed because of the coronavirus pandemic in 2020 and has not reopened. (WSPC.)

Seven

KENTUCKY RIVER

The Kentucky River became an important transportation route beginning in 1787 when Gen. James Wilkinson took a flatboat loaded with tobacco, hams, and butter to New Orleans by way of the Ohio and Mississippi Rivers. John Halley of Boonesborough guided his flatboats full of produce to New Orleans in 1789 and 1791. Flatboats like these left Boonesborough every spring until the Civil War disrupted commerce on the river. (AC.)

Steamboats began traveling the Kentucky River in the early 1800s. Construction of the lock and dam system eventually allowed year-round travel of commercial and pleasure craft up and down the river. The *Martha*, a gas-powered sternwheel tugboat, is shown pushing a coal barge downriver in the 1930s. The road seen behind the *Martha* provides access to the ferry on the Clark County side of the river. (DWC.)

Richard Roe, a sternwheel steamboat packet, made her last voyage up the Kentucky River in 1921, making stops at Monterey, Frankfort, Boonesborough, and other ports. A smaller packet, *Vim*, was rebuilt and christened *Richard Roe* in 1919. She worked the packet trade carrying passengers and freight between Louisville and Madison, Indiana, except for periodic excursions up the Kentucky River. (WFP.)

This limestone cliff, located about a half mile downstream from Boonesborough, marks the beginning of the Kentucky River palisades. Between this point and Frankfort, the river channel cuts a 100-mile gorge through the Bluegrass region. At the base of these palisades, one finds the oldest exposed rocks in Kentucky, formed during the Ordovician Period about 450 million years ago. (AC.)

Planners projected that the Kentucky River lock and dam system, completed in 1917, would be a boon to commercial traffic on the river. They expected the coal industry to benefit from cheaper rates than the railroads were charging. As it turned out, very little coal was ever hauled on the Kentucky River. Extensive commercial use of the river, such as moving sand barges as shown here, never materialized. (WSPC.)

The Kentucky River palisades provide a nearly inexhaustible commercial supply of Ordovician Period limestone. Rock from the Camp Nelson formation has been extensively mined at Boonesborough. This abandoned limestone quarry on the Clark County side was operated in the 1930s and 1940s by J.A. Fries & Company of Knoxville, Tennessee; Caldwell Stone Company of Danville; and finally, by the Allen-Codell Company of Clark County. A rock crusher (above) stands very close to the road, which itself skirts very close to the river. The quarry high wall (below) today stands as a landmark on Athens-Boonesborough Road about a mile downstream from Boonesborough. (Both, UK.)

The Admiral's Day celebration began at Frankfort in 1963. The Admirals were boating enthusiasts who met annually to publicize state programs designed to develop Kentucky's waterways. The festivities included a boat parade and picnic. The celebration moved to the new Fort Boonesborough State Park in 1967. On the Sunday before Labor Day, boats gathered at Clay's Ferry, south of Lexington, and traveled six miles upriver to Boonesborough Beach. The boats, ranging from large cruisers to small canoes, docked at the beach, and a picnic for the public commenced. Other high points of the day included prizes for boats and a beauty contest. The views here from the late 1970s demonstrate the multitude of boats and great crowds of attendees. (Both, WSPC.)

Admiral's Day prizes were awarded for boats in several categories. The award for the best-decorated runabout in 1976 (above) was Ed Anderkin's "Water Wagon," which was fitted out like a covered wagon pulled by an attached wooden steer. His boat was edged with authentic hand-hewn wood sideboards and rustic iron fittings. Judges selected as the best pontoon boat Kenneth Eason's "Heart of Dixie," a one-man craft propelled by a rear paddlewheel (below). Eason, of Lexington, returned to the river several times to take the prize with his jury-rigged boat. (Both, WSPC.)

A much-anticipated event was the annual Admiral's Day beauty contest, which usually drew dozens of contestants. Pictured above from left to right are the winners of the Miss Kentucky Admiral contest, ages 16 to 21, Nancy Raque, 1975 winner; Mary Barnett, 1976 winner; Karen Hale, first runner-up; and Linda Stinnett, second runner-up. Below are the Junior Miss Kentucky Admiral winners, ages 12 to 15: Andrea Coleman, 1975 winner; Kathy Coleman, 1976 winner; Sarah Gibson, first runner-up; and Jennifer Baker, second runner-up. In other years, the contests went by the names of Miss Kentucky River and Little Miss Kentucky River. (Both, WSPC.)

Other Admiral's Day festivities included water skiing exhibitions, canoe races, talent contests, swimming contests, and children's games. Up to 100 boats participated in the parade, and in the late 1960s and early 1970s, the crowds numbered from 5,000 to 10,000 people. Live entertainment, a popular feature in the 1970s, featured local groups like Sand 'n' Rock (left). A large crowd (below) watches the entertainment stage from seating in front of the bathhouse. After the US Army Corps of Engineers decommissioned the locks in 1990, participation in Admiral's Day greatly diminished. The last celebration was held in 1994. (Both, WSPC.)

The 1975 prize for the best-decorated cruiser went to Frank Hobson's "Lill Tiki." A Hawaiian warrior stands at the front of the top deck, and a bevy of hula dancers in grass skirts perform in the rear. Note the three fake palm trees. Prizes were also awarded for the most unique boat and for traveling the greatest distance. (WSPC.)

Jim, Oliver, and Bert Shearer removed the 10-foot, cherry-wood pilot's wheel from the *O.F. Shearer* sternwheel towboat. The boat was built for Dravo Corporation as the *Victory* in 1919, sold to O.F. Shearer & Sons in 1939, and dismantled after an accident in 1952. The Shearer family of Boonesborough operated a successful commercial barge business on the Kentucky and Ohio Rivers. (WSPC.)

The Kentucky River near Boonesborough, a popular swimming spot, was the site of numerous drownings over the years. Victims were most often young swimmers or fishermen who could not swim when their boat overturned. Clark County sheriff Leonard Lawson stands at the rear of a US Coast Guard boat as rescuers search for Timothy Richards, who disappeared while swimming there with friends in July 1978. (WSPC.)

The first Boathouse, owned by Cain Gibson of Lexington, opened near Ford in early May 1972. The small floating restaurant built on a barge had only been in business for about two weeks when it sank in the river near the bank. The cause of the incident was not reported. Cranes finally raised the boat five days later. Local people do not recall that the Boathouse ever reopened. (WSPC.)

A memorable floating restaurant in the Boonesborough area during the 1970s was the Sandpiper, a social club with beer, whiskey, dancing, and a fancy clientele. It was fitted out with a kitchen, bar, dining room, wall-to-wall carpets, fireplace, and a canopy over the deck. The Sandpiper mysteriously sank in 1979, was raised, sank again, and today lies just beneath the surface of the Three Trees Canoe-Kayak boat dock. (BT.)

Linville Puckett's Settler's Cabin restaurant, shown here under construction in 1978, was located on the Kentucky River in Clark County just downstream from the Boonesborough Bridge. Puckett (second from the left) had been a star basketball player at Clark County and played for Adolph Rupp at the University of Kentucky. (WSPC.)

Riverview Marina was one of the last large boat docks to operate near Boonesborough. The owner, Kentucky native Fernando Cress, purchased a trailer park in 1988 and installed a boat dock just downstream from the present Three Trees Canoe-Kayak's dock. In 1992, Cress opened a floating restaurant here called the Boathouse. It was a barge with a frame two-story dining room and kitchen and a one-story covered dining pavilion. He sold the restaurant to Dr. Timothy Dineen in 2007. The Boathouse became run down and then burned in an April 2010 fire that also consumed the marina's wood decking. The remaining steel frame of the marina washed away in a flood the following month. (Both, NC.)

The legendary riverman Johnny Allman (1906–1989) rose in the ranks of the Kentucky State Police before getting into the restaurant business. In 1944, he and Charlie Stevens leased and operated the Boonesboro Beach Resort. After several years Allman opened his own restaurant overlooking the river, about two miles north of Boonesborough on Athens-Boonesboro Road (below). He specialized in catfish, sirloin steaks, and beer. He also introduced two innovations still popular today: fried banana peppers and beer cheese. Allman sold his restaurant and opened at a new location across the road at the site where Hall's Restaurant stands today. His businesses suffered many floods and several fires before his retirement in 1978. (Both, WSPC.)

113

Two miles north of Boonesborough stands the oldest establishment on the river, Halls Restaurant. Johnny Allman had an eatery here that he sold to Carl Johnson. George and Gertrude Hall purchased the restaurant in 1965, and it burned shortly after. They rebuilt, and their son Steve ran it from 1970 until his death in 1988. Now known as Hall's On The River, the restaurant still serves beer cheese and fried banana peppers. (WSPC.)

At the Clark County end of the Boonesborough bridge stood a small log cabin tavern called the Daniel Boone Inn (DBI). Behind the inn were two outhouses, with one marked "Gentlemen" and one marked "Ladies." At the border of a wet county and a dry county, the DBI advertised itself as "The Last Chance" and as "The First Chance," depending on which direction one crossed the bridge. (DWC.)

The 65-foot *Dixie Belle* carrying 150 passengers sails downstream from Boonesborough in 1979. In 1976, Capt. James Cross of Winchester brought this sternwheeler to Boonesborough where he conducted summer river excursions through 1981. In the 1982 season, Cross moved to Shaker Landing to take advantage of the growing tourist trade at Shakertown. Due to the rising costs of the aging riverboat, excursions ended with the 2021 season. (DWC.)

In 1960, Capt. John Donaldson purchased the *Brooklyn* for commercial trade on the Kentucky River. In the 1970s, Linville Puckett acquired the boat for a beer depot he opened across from Fort Boonesborough. After it sank, Eddie Carter purchased the boat, raised it in 1986, and moved it downriver, where it sank again. The sternwheel tugboat now rests partly submerged near the bank, a little below Hall's Restaurant. (WSPC.)

The Kentucky River is subject to frequent floods that cause considerable damage to homes and businesses located along its banks. The 1937 flood was one of the worst ever recorded. Shown here is the hotel at the Boonesboro Beach Resort surrounded by floodwaters. Notice the porch posts made of trimmed cedar logs. (WFC.)

Two "river rats," Bob Tabor and Angie "Reg" Campbell, go for a joyride on the Kentucky River near Hall's Restaurant during the 1978 flood. The pair are shown paddling a 12-foot aluminum Sportspal canoe. The water level at Lock 10 crested at 40.15 feet, the highest ever recorded on the Kentucky River. (WSPC.)

The March 1994 Kentucky River flood was caused by a major ice storm followed by heavy rains that swelled river levels. At Fort Boonesborough State Park, water completely covered the beach and soaked the first level of the bathhouse. Floods frequently cause the beach and campground to close, and sometimes the entire park has to shut down. (WSPC.)

The flood of March 2021 was the second-highest ever recorded on the Kentucky River. It crested at Boonesborough at 38 feet, 12 feet above flood stage. Hall's Restaurant (at left center) suffered extensive damage and was closed for over a year. Athens-Boonesboro Road in front of the restaurant was blocked for days. After four days of rain, rising waters washed out several Clark County roads. (WH.)

Ford, located a mile up the river from Boonesborough, grew rapidly after the railroad reached there in 1883, and a number of sawmills followed. The largest operation was the massive Burt & Brabb Lumber Company, shown here, with a capacity to produce 15 million board feet per year. The mills slowed after the Corps of Engineers required logs to be rafted and finally closed after the railroad came to towns farther upriver. (AC.)

In 1883, Kentucky Central Railroad constructed a line from Winchester to Richmond that crossed the Kentucky River at Ford, which proved a boon to the town's lumber industry. This photograph shows the bridge over the river and the opening of a tunnel on the Madison County side. L&N Railroad acquired the line soon after it opened and still operates freight service over it today. (WSPC.)

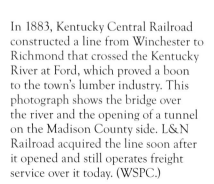

The Ford Post Office was established in 1883. By 1900, Ford had several stores and churches, a hotel, a school, and a jail. With a population of 1,200, it was pushing Winchester to become the largest city in Clark County. Opal Warner, who was postmistress from 1961 until her retirement in 1989, operated the post office out of Warner's Grocery. The post office closed in 2004. (WSPC.)

In 1954, the character of Ford changed dramatically with the construction of the William C. Dale coal-fired power station. Its four generating units, rated at 196 megawatts, produced electricity for East Kentucky Power, which supplied 16 Kentucky rural electric cooperatives. Due to its age and increasingly stringent air-quality regulations, the plant closed in 2016 and has since been dismantled. (WSPC.)

The first "Kentucky River Sweep" cleanup event was held in September 1991. Here, volunteers load a discarded pipe onto a boat from a Clark County riverbank. About 1,000 volunteers in 19 counties sweated in 90-degree heat to clean up old tires, discarded appliances, and other trash along the river. The event, coordinated by the Kentucky River Authority, became an annual affair and continues today. (WSPC.)

Kentucky River Watershed Watch (KRWW) staff train 4H volunteers in Clark County. The KRWW conducts regular sampling and monitoring in order to improve and protect the water quality of the Kentucky River. They work with the Kentucky Division of Water and other organizations to track river trends for *E. coli*, pH, dissolved oxygen, metals, nitrogen, and phosphorus. (KRWW.)

Eight

MODERN BOONESBOROUGH

Boonesborough has seen many changes over the last 50 years. One highlight is the Daniel Boone Heritage Trail, now designated a Kentucky Scenic Byway. The route begins on Athens-Boonesboro Road (KY 418) across the river from Fort Boonesborough and continues seven miles to Athens, where Daniel Boone established Boone Station in 1779. Scenic byways have viewsheds worthy of preservation, restoration, protection, and enhancement. (AC.)

Fort Boonesborough State Park has seen a number of ups and downs. The campground now has a central service building with showers, restrooms, and laundry facilities. There is also a camp grocery (shown here), picnic shelters, tables, grills, and a playground. The swimming pool, which closed during the COVID-19 pandemic, has not reopened due to serious repair issues. The flood of 2021 practically destroyed the famed Boonesborough Beach. (AC.)

The monument in front of the fort, installed by the Society of Boonesborough, is inscribed with names of the men and women who were Boonesborough pioneers. The society has also provided additional interpretive signage at the park. The fort is open for tours from April through October and still features first-person interpretation of 18th-century life and period craft demonstrations. (AC.)

The old lockhouses and outbuildings at the Corps of Engineers reservation at Boonesborough, now owned by the Kentucky River Authority, were restored in 1996. The upper lockhouse opened as the Kentucky River Museum in 2002. Jenimarie Sowers, the granddaughter of John Walters Sr., until recently served as a tour guide at the museum, which provides visitors with an insight into the lives of the Walters family who worked here for more than 70 years. (AC.)

Lock 10 permanently closed at the end of 1994. The Corps of Engineers deeded the lock and dam to the state in 1996. It is now owned by the Kentucky River Authority, which had the lock sealed with concrete. In a four-year, $26 million project completed in 2021, KRA had the dam rehabilitated with the construction of eight concrete-filled, steel-sheet pile cellular structures upstream of the existing auxiliary dam. The original dam was not raised. (AC.)

Since the permanent closure of Lock 10 at Boonesborough, recreational craft have been confined to the pools above or below the dam. The once numerous river marinas have mostly disappeared. Jason Harris (pictured above) and his wife, Nathalie, operate Old Habits Bar and Grill Boat Dock and boat launch in the pool above the dam. The dock, located near the mouth of Twomile Creek about three miles upstream from Boonesborough, is accessed by Ford Road. Jeff and Angel Cress have a dock at their business, Three Trees Canoe-Kayak Rental and RV Park (below), located a quarter of a mile below the Boonesborough Bridge. The dock, accessible via Athens-Boonesboro Road, has free launching for small boats. (Both, AC.)

Across the river from Fort Boonesborough State Park, near the town of Ford, is the site of the Civil War Fort at Boonesboro. The earthenworks here were manned by African American troops in 1863–1865 to defend this strategic Kentucky River crossing from Confederate raiders. A self-guided trail leads to the hilltop where the fort stood. The parking area has a series of murals painted by Winchester artist Phil May. The works depict the history of the Boonesborough area from the era of the Adena people of prehistoric Clark County up through modern times. The example below depicts the old Boonesborough ferry. (Both, AC.)

Lower Howard's Creek Nature & Heritage Preserve consists of 441 acres in Clark County. The Preserve is home to endangered and rare plants and irreplaceable historical and archaeological features. A 228-acre tract was dedicated as a state nature preserve in 2001. The primary purposes of the preserve are to protect rare species, protect and interpret historical/archaeological resources, conduct scientific research, protect and restore natural communities, and foster environmental education. The main entrance, shown above, is on Athens-Boonesboro Road. The 2.8-mile John Holder Trail, adjacent to Hall's Restaurant, opened with a ribbon cutting in 2012. Pictured below are, from left to right, volunteer Bill Crankshaw, holding a walking stick; Henry Branham, county judge-executive; Clare Sipple, preserve manager; Joyce Bender, state nature preserves; Joe Dietz of Kentucky Heritage Lands. (Both, AC.)

BIBLIOGRAPHY

Draper, Lyman C. *Life of Daniel Boone*. Ted Franklin Belue, editor. Mechanicsburg, PA: Stackpole Books, 1998.

Jones, Randell. *In the Footsteps of Daniel Boone*. Winston-Salem, NC: John F. Blair, Publisher, 2005.

Hammon, Neal O., and James Russell Harris. "Daniel Boone the Businessman: Revising the Myth of Failure." *Register of the Kentucky Historical Society* (Winter 2014):5-50.

Ranck, George W. *Boonesborough*. Louisville, KY: Filson Club Publications, 1901.

O'Malley, Nancy. *Boonesborough Unearthed*. Lexington, KY: University Press of Kentucky, 2019.

Verhoeff, Mary. *Kentucky River Navigation*. Louisville, KY: Filson Club Publications, 1917.

Johnson, Leland R., and Charles E. Parrish. *Kentucky River Development: The Commonwealth's Waterway*. Louisville, KY: Louisville Engineer District, US Army Corps of Engineers, 1999.

DISCOVER THOUSANDS OF LOCAL HISTORY BOOKS
FEATURING MILLIONS OF VINTAGE IMAGES

Arcadia Publishing, the leading local history publisher in the United States, is committed to making history accessible and meaningful through publishing books that celebrate and preserve the heritage of America's people and places.

Find more books like this at
www.arcadiapublishing.com

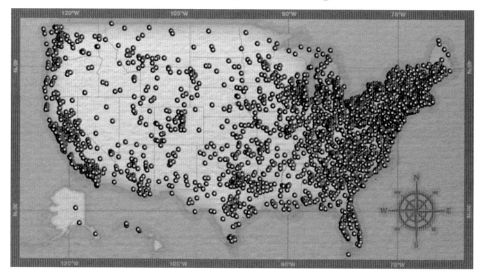

Search for your hometown history, your old stomping grounds, and even your favorite sports team.